THE SOCIAL WAGE

Its Role under Capitalism
and in the Transition from
Socialism to Communism

by Ernie Trory

HOVE, EAST SUSSEX:
Crabtree Press Limited
4 Portland Avenue
1992

© Ernie Trory 1992

First Published 1992
by Crabtree Press Ltd.

Typeset by Pleckbond Ltd. (TU)
119/121 Falcon Road
London SW11 2PQ

Made and Printed in Great Britain
by BPCC Wheatons Ltd. (TU), Exeter

Cover Design by Steve Flanders

ISBN 0 9515098 1 0

Introduction

IN MODERN CAPITALIST SOCIETY employees receive their wages in two parts. The first part is the money wage. That is the cash a wage-worker receives in his or her pay-packet at the end of the week or month. In theory this is spent at the will of the recipient, although most, if not all, will be used to discharge such commitments as rent or mortgage repayments, food and clothing for the family, gas and electricity bills, bus and train fares or car expenses, telephone bills and, of course, taxes. For the average worker, the amount left over to be spent really freely varies from nil to very little. Employers of labour, and those living on the interest of past profits, as well as those living on rents, also pay taxes, usually considerably higher than those paid by individual wage-workers beacuse of their greater incomes. All of the moneys collected in taxes, whether from employees or their employers, go into general funds from which social wages are dispensed in the form of local and national social services.

In many of its categories, the social wage is paid, not to all and sundry, but to those in need. These include young children, the sick, the aged and the unemployed. The low-paid are also included and qualify for rent rebates and sometimes for other concessions. Free or subsidised medical treatment and education are also part of the social wage, as are the upkeep of public parks, subsidised bus and rail travel, street cleaning and refuse collection.

There are many other categories, some of them of doubtful value, but the above will suffice to explain what is generally meant by the social wage as distinct from the money wage.

In Britain, part of the social wage is sometimes referred to as the "Welfare State," though I took exception to this description when, in 1984, I was asked to deliver the *Third Tommy Jackson Memorial Lecture* on this subject. I pointed out that "state welfare" would have been a more accurate description. During the course of the lecture, I went into the subject in detail; and since I can think of no better way of describing the role of the social wage under capitalism, I am publishing the lecture, exactly as I delivered it, as the first part of this study. Apart from adding a footnote, rendered necessary by the defection of the socialist countries from the principles enshrined in the works of Marx and Engels, I have neither altered nor added a single word.

The second part of the book deals with the role of the social wage in the period of transition from socialism to communism and tentatively offers the suggestion that one of the key mistakes that ultimately led to the collapse of the socialist community of nations in Europe was the failure of the communist and workers parties concerned to convince their members, and through them the workers in the factories and fields, of the importance of the social wage. Their failure to activate the populations of their countries in the implementation of a policy recognising this led to an over-valuation of the money wage and was partly responsible for the development of an obsession for consumerism.

For some time I had been concerned with this obsession in the socialist countries. I could easily see that by taking the access to consumer goods (available to the higher paid workers in the capitalist countries at the expense of the lower paid) as a yardstick, and ignoring the greater basic advantages of the higher social wage for the whole population in the socialist countries, a distorted view of the two systems of society could lead to a demand for a return to a market economy. But it was not until I read Mick James's review of Carlos Tablada's *Che Guevara: Economics and Politics in the Transition to Socialism,* in the *New Worker* on the 30th November, 1990, and later Tablada's book itself, that I realised why it was so important to win the people of a socialist country, even in the earliest stages of its development, for a conscious realisation of the importance of the social wage as a moral incentive to balance the necessary material incentive of the money wage; and in the later stages, during the transition from socialism to communism, of the need for the social wage to take precedence over the money wage, even to the extent, eventually, of the total disappearance of the latter. It is hoped that the second part of this book will be sufficient to stimulate a discussion on this important issue. I ask no more than that.

As an afterthought, I have included a four-part *Appendix* reproducing two speeches and two articles of mine that show how my own doubts about the legitimacy of the policies pursued by Gorbachev were first aroused in 1987 and how they developed into total opposition as the events that led to the subsequent crisis unfolded. This might help others to clarify their own positions.

23rd March, 1992.

THE WELFARE STATE

The Third
Tommy Jackson Annual Memorial Lecture
Delivered in Crawley at the AEU Hall
on the 23rd May, 1984.

FIRST LET ME SAY what a great honour it is to be asked to deliver this lecture under the auspices of the Tommy Jackson Memorial Committee. I had the pleasure of meeting TAJ, as he liked to be called, on one or two occasions in the late 'thirties and of hearing him speak. Once, when he spoke in the old Labour Club in London Road, Brighton, I took along a copy of his *Dialectics,* on the flyleaf of which I had pasted a picture of him taken from an advertisement for his book. I asked him to sign it and he wrote, under his picture: "This hurts me more than it hurts you." The subject of his lecture was "Dialectical Materialism" and I remember his imploring us to regard it as something more than "just a phrase that rolls trippingly off the tongue." I have treasured that book ever since and I have it with me here today.

In her centenary appreciation of Tommy Jackson, his daughter, Vivien Morton, quotes her father as having prophesied: "I shall die an old bum, loved but unrespected." It is true that his appearance, in spite of the efforts of his loving wife, Lydia, to whom he dedicated his great book, *Dialectics,* was of "an unkempt scholar. It is true that he was loved, perhaps for his eccentricities rather than in spite of them. But it is not true that he died unrespected. The hundreds of tributes sent in his name to the *Daily Worker* after his death on the 18th August, 1955, is a measure of the esteem in which he was held. That respect can only grow as his works become better known and as these annual memorial lectures increase in importance with the passing of the years.

In its wisdom, the Tommy Jackson Memorial Committee has asked me to speak on the subject of the "welfare state." This is not as easy as it sounds. Before one can speak on such a subject, one must first define it. It is a fact that in all the mass of reading on the "welfare state," I have yet to come across an adequate definition of it. My own definition would be: "that state in which the welfare of the whole of its people is paramount." That is not a situation that applies in this country at the present time; nor did it apply here at any time in the past.

If we take the state to be, as Marx described it, an organ of class rule, "an organ for the oppression of one class by another," then we must ask of any state

THE SOCIAL WAGE

described as a "welfare state," as, indeed, Lenin would have done: "Whose welfare? Whose state?" It follows automatically that the answer to the first question depends upon the answer to the second. In a capitalist society, the so-called "welfare state" exists for the welfare of the capitalist class. Since this class is a small minority of the total population, such a state cannot be described as a true "welfare state." Only a socialist state can be so described.

What is actually meant, however, when we refer today to the "welfare state" is, in fact, the "state welfare" that is dispensed through the major services of education, health, housing and social security, including unemployment benefits, redundancy pay, pensions, family allowances etc. The "welfare state" in Britain today is a euphemism for the system of "Social Insurance and Allied Services" investigated in 1942 by a committee headed by Beveridge (a Liberal); incorporated in a White Paper by Willinck (Tory Minister of Health) in 1944; and brought into being by Aneurin Bevan (Labour Minister of Health) in 1946. I will return to the subject of the true "welfare state" later. In the meantime, let us take a brief look at the history of "state welfare" in Britain.

Up until the end of the 19th century, the only "welfare" available was dispensed under the Poor Law, introduced in 1601 by Elizabeth I. In his *A People's History of England*, A. L. Morton, who is Tommy Jackson's son-in-law, tells us:

> During the 18th century the Poor Law had been based on the principle that a person was entitled to relief in the parish where he had been born and nowhere else. In practice this meant that all the poor were regarded as paupers and were liable to be deported to their place of birth on the suspicion that at some future date they might become chargeable upon the rates.

By 1720, there was a widespread movement for the erection of workhouses, where it was found that the poor could be maintained at less than half the expense of their weekly relief. It was not until 1834, however, that it was made compulsory by law for those receiving public assistance because of their inability to work, to enter a workhouse. The sick were included in this category and so were cared for, after a fashion, inside the workhouses. Many hospitals are still housed in old workhouses. A good example is the General Hospital in Elm Grove, Brighton. This was a workhouse when I first came to live in the town.

As the system developed, more and bigger workhouses were built, not by single parishes but by groups of parishes, sometimes as many as twenty, known as "unions." Conditions in these workhouses were grim. The food was poor and the inmates were subjected to such senseless and degrading tasks as oakum picking and stone breaking. Perhaps the most heartless condition was the separation of the sexes, which meant that elderly couples were forced to live apart in their declining years. In the words of the Poor Law Commission of 1834, the inmates of workhouses were "subjected to such courses of labour and discipline as will repel the indolent and vicious." The workhouses became known as Poor Law bastilles.

But not everyone agreed that the poor should receive any assistance at all. In his *Theory of Population*, Malthus wrote: "As the population unceasingly tends to overstep the means of subsistance, benevolence is folly, a public encouragement to poverty. The state can do nothing in the face of this natural law but leave poverty to its fate. At best it can make death easier for the poor." Commented Karl Marx:

> With this amiable theory the English Parliament combines the opinion that pauperism is the sort of poverty for which the worker himself is responsible, and which therefore must not be regarded as a misfortune but rather suppressed as a crime. Thus arose the workhouse system ... whose internal arrangements deter the poverty-stricken from seeking refuge from starvation. In the workhouse are ingeniously combined benevolence and revenge of the bourgeoisie upon such of the poor as appeal to its benevolence.

Tommy Jackson, in his *Dialectics*, quotes Marx as saying that: "England first attempted to destroy pauperism by benevolence and administrative measures; then attributed the progressive increase in paupersim, not to the growth of modern industry, but to its own Poor Law; then, finally, after attempts in reforming the administration of public benevolence had failed to check the growth of pauperism, treated it as a fault of the poor and punished it accordingly." To which Tommy Jackson added his own comments as follows:

> Nearly a century later, we can read Marx's argument and marvel at his foresight. The treatment of the typically modern form of paupersim, mass unemployment, has followed historically exactly the same line. first, in the period 1885-1905, an attempt was made to destroy it by benevolence and administrative measures: Lord Mayors' funds, Salvation Army and Church Army work depots and farm colonies and Labour Exchanges. Then an attempt was made to cure the defects of this system by the organised state benevolence of the Unemployment Insurance Acts and their careful administration. Finally, as the numbers of the unemployed continued to grow, an outcry was raised against the "dole" as the cause of unemployment, against the unemployed as "professional dole-drawers" ... and in consequence came the "Means Test."

THE SOCIAL WAGE

It does not need much imagination to project this analysis still further into the future until we come to our own times, when once again mass unemployment is on the order of the day and when the unemployed are continually blamed for their laziness. If we substitute "unemployment" for "pauperism" in the following passage, written by Marx in 1844, it will read as well today as it did then:

> The general significance attained by pauperism in England consists precisely in the fact that in spite of all administrative measures, pauperism has, in the course of development, grown into a national institution. It has become, inevitably, the subject of an extensive and ramified administration; which administration, however, no longer aims at extinguishing it, but only of disciplining it in perpetuity.

In 1831, the first of the great cholera epidemics swept the country. This represented a threat, not only to the vast urban communities living in squalor and degradation in the shadow of the factories, but to the ruling class itself. It seems that the cholera germs did not know their place. They attacked rich and poor alike, although it must be said that the rich were better equipped to withstand their attacks. Nevertheless, the first Public Health Act came into being in 1848. Supported by the trade unions and by the Chartists, as well as by the more far-seeing factory and mill owners, it was bitterly opposed by the medical establishment and by the water companies. But as Sir Edwin Chadwick, a forthright sanitary reformer, explained: "If a Chartist millenium were to be averted, the governing classes must free the governed from the sharp spur on their misery by improving the physical conditions of their lives."

It was in that year that Marx and Engels wrote in *The Manifesto of the Communist Party:* "A part of the bourgeoisie is desirous of redressing social grievances in order to secure the continued existence of bourgeois society." I cannot help but compare the comments of Chadwick and of Marx and Engels with the remarks made in a broadcast by Clement Attlee on the death, in 1951, of Ernest Bevin, whom Attlee credited with having held to the view that "there must always be a positive policy of raising standards of living throughout the world so as to destroy the conditions in which Russian communism thrives."

Thanks largely to the struggles of the organised working class for better conditions in the factories and for better conditions generally, the Poor Law system was merged with the public health services during the 1870s and the Public Health Act of 1895 ushered in a system that is still with us today.

It was the Friendly Societies, however, notably in South Wales among the miners, that were responsible for the introduction of a scheme for personal health

THE WELFARE STATE

care under the "club" system. In 1804 there were a million members of Friendly Societies in Britain but by 1900 there were seven million. In 1911, Lloyd George institutionalised this system under the National Health Insurance Act, which set up the "panel" system. It was not completely altruistic. The ruling class needed a healthy workforce and a healthy fighting population to carry on its wars of colonial expansion. Later, towards the end of the so-called "Great War," it was revealed that only one in three was fit for military service, but it was not until 1919 that the Ministry of Health was set up.

Similar historical developments had also taken place in the advanced countries of Europe during the last quarter of the 19th century. In fact, it was Bismarck, Chancellor of Prussia, who most deserved to be known as the "father of state welfare." It was he who legislated for insurance against sickness in 1883, against accident in 1884, and against old age in 1889. Somewhere along the line, he also managed to nationalise the German railways. In 1890 he was dismissed by the young Kaiser Wilhelm II, who nevertheless promoted the Workmen's Protection Act of 1891. This dealt with the conditions in factories against a background of rising industrialism after the unification of Germany in 1871, when it was said that "the chimneys grew like mushrooms." This was especially so after Bismarck had gone over to tariff protection, or what we would now call "import controls," in 1879.

Marxist socialism also grew rapidly in this fruitful soil. Bismarck combatted it with repressive laws, despite that he is sometimes referred to as "one of the greatest socialists of his day." He was, in fact, a perfect example of that section of the bourgeoisie that Marx spoke of as being "desirous of redressing social grievances in order to secure the continued existence of bourgeois society."

The aftermath of the Second World War gave a new impetus to "welfarism," which manifested itself in Britain in the Beveridge Report. The findings of the committee set up to investigate the possibility of instituting a comprehensive scheme for "Social Insurance and Allied Services" were published towards the end of 1942. In an article in the January, 1943 issue of *Labour Monthly*, William Gallacher, then a Communist Member of Parliament, wrote: "The long-awaited Beveridge Report is now in circulation, and various forces will soon be lining up for and against."

According to the Employers' Federation, "social services involving a heavy tax on industry were the cause of much unemployment, owing to the heavy handicap they place on foreign trade." Said Gallacher: "Had it not been for the social services, the population would have been almost wiped out and capitalist industry would have come to a standstill. The social services have not only been a measure of insurance for the health of the people, they have also been a form, and a very necessary form, of insurance for the profits of the employers. There are no profits obtained from the residents of a sanatorium or the occupants of

THE SOCIAL WAGE

a cemetary."

In his report, Beveridge revealed that under the then existing system, more than a third of the money paid in for insurance went in administration. The insurance companies had a total of 80,000 employees, most of them collectors. Gallacher feared that all they would see, if an all-embracing national insurance scheme came into being, would be that they would be thrown out of a job. It would be necessary to explain to them the advantages that would accrue to everyone if it could be implemented.

Gallacher saw the possibilities of a fully comprehensive health scheme. His own ideas, however, were considerably in advance of those envisaged in the Beveridge Report. "For all large factories," he wrote, "or for a group of adjacent small factories or pits, it will be necessary to establish full-functioning clinics with competent medical men in attendance." This was based on the three "assumptions," upon which, according to Beveridge, the scheme depended. The first of these was: "comprehensive health and rehabilitation services for prevention and cure of disease and restoration of capacity for work, available to all members of the community." The second "assumption" was allowances for every child after the first. And the third "assumption" was: "Maintenance of employment, that is to say, avoidance of mass unemployment." Gallacher thought that the third "assumption" would determine all the rest.

When asked in the House of Commons, by a visitor, what he thought of the proposed scheme as outlined in the Beveridge Report, Gallacher admitted that he had reservations but said he would support it. "Yes," said the visitor, "it's a good foundation." "No," replied Gallacher, "it's not a foundation at all; it's part of the superstructure and it won't stand up unless it has a good foundation under it." Gallacher thought that with mass unemployment, it would fall to pieces. How right he was. The scheme was part of the superstructure of capitalism. It would work in the initial period of post-war reconstruction, while unemployment was low, but when unemployment began to assume mass proportions again it would collapse. Gallacher believed that the only "good foundation" would be a socialist one. "The right to exploit the people for profit," he wrote, "cannot be tolerated if there is to be social security."

Sir William Beveridge's own views on the subject were set out in a book entitled *Full employment in a Free Society*, which was published in the autumn of 1944. In it he comes to the conclusion that in an "unplanned market economy, even apart from cyclical depression, there may be chronic or nearly chronic deficiency in the total demand for labour." For those of you not familiar with this type of circumlocution, it means that in a capitalist economy, even apart from periodic slumps, there may still be mass unemployment or near mass unemployment. He avoids any reference to the nationalisation of industries, which he regarded as a separate issue, and talks of the "expansion of the public sector of business, so as to enlarge the area within which investment can be stabilised directly." But as Emile Burns pointed out in a review of Beveridge's book, in the December, 1944 issue of *Labour Monthly:*

> Crisis and unemployment . . . are a product of capitalist production. They can only be eliminated, short of a complete change to socialism, by the most drastic interference with the normal work of capitalism. It is necessary to be clear on this. The effective measures, which Beveridge proposes to cure unemployment, are not measures to bolster up capitalism, but measures to interfere with capitalism, to bring the political power of the people to bear in such a way that capital is unable to follow its own laws, and is compelled to serve the people. It is a political issue of controlling capitalism; it is not a question of changing the spots of the leopard or the heart of the monopolist.

During the war capitalism had to be controlled to a certain extent in its own interests. But even then, for all the fortunes made by the capitalists, it proved to be extraordinarily difficult. In peacetime it would be impossible. Said Emile Burns in his review:

> Beveridge uses the orthodox capitalist economic approach. He steadfastly avoids the term "capital" and therefore cannot make a clear analysis. Instead of "capital," he speaks of "savings" and "investment." Following the mystical phrases of Keynes, he credits people with a greater or lesser "propensity to consume" or "propensity to save" or "propensity to invest." The turnover of capital is broken up into these mystical "propensities." He seems unaware that the "propensity to consume" for the great majority of people is determined by the circulation of capital itself; it is the variable capital. Capitalist production is for surplus value, which has first to be realised on the market and then "accumulated" and used as new capital to produce more surplus value. It is the laws of the circulation of capital that contain the key to relative over- production and crises; it is no good looking for it in the "propensities" of individuals. Analyses based on such "propensities" are pure mystifications.

In 1944, Willinck, Tory Minister of Health, produced a White Paper for a national health service, free at time of use, centrally directed but administered by local authorities. In July, 1945, a Labour government was elected, with a huge overall majority, pledged to a programme of radical social reform. In January, 1946, Aneurin Bevan, the new Minister of Health, presented an outline of the new service to the British Medical Association. A Bill was duly processed

THE SOCIAL WAGE

through Parliament and in November, 1946, it received the Royal assent. There were numerous weaknesses in the service. Doctors and consultants were allowed to keep their private practices, even when they opted to join the National Health Service. Worst of all, the private drug companies retained their monopoly of the production of all medicines prescribed. They should have been nationalised at the outset. For years, Valium, produced for as little as £20 per kilogram, was sold to the National Health Service for £1,962 per kilogram.[1] In 1970 alone, doctors in Britain wrote nearly five and a half million prescriptions for Valium. This is but one example of how the National Health Service benefited the privately owned drugs companies.

The National Health Service, a major part of the so-called "welfare state," was a scheme for social insurance based on benefits in return for contributions. It had to be sound actuarily, which meant it did nothing to redistribute wealth in real terms. It was, of course, of great temporary benefit to the lower-paid sections of the working class, to the chronically sick, to the old age pensioners and to the unemployed. It took from the fully employed in the form of compulsory contributions and taxation of wages in order to do so. In that sense it did redistribute some of the "wealth" of the better paid workers among the worse paid. But there was no significant resdistribution of the wealth of the employing class among the working class.

By 1947, Britain was already in the throes of an economic crisis that heralded the beginning of the breakdown of the much-lauded "welfare state," even before it had been properly instituted. The Labour leaders blamed the war. In their *ABC of the Crisis* they claimed that the 1939-45 war had been "seven times more destructive than the 1914-18 war." In an election broadcast in October, 1951, Attlee said: "In the war, we sold most of our investments and had to allow export trade to fall away. During the war, American lease-lend aid freed us from anxiety. When peace returned, we were faced with the stark reality of the situation."

It has to be said, however, that the country that suffered most of all the Allies during the Second World War, was the Soviet Union, and, next to that country, the countries of eastern Europe. Yet all these countries had shown striking recoveries and considerable advances in production and living standards. According to the United Nations Monthly Bulletin of Statistics for 1952, taking the index number of all National Incomes at 100 in 1938, these had increased by 1951 to the following: France 106, Britain 113, Czechoslovakia 138, Poland 169, the USA 198 and the USSR 224. The USA, of course, was capitalising on

---

[1] According to Cutting the Welfare State: Who Profits? Published by Counter Information Services, 5 Poland Street, London W1.

THE WELFARE STATE

the profits it had made during the Second World War, from which it had emerged relatively unscathed.

No, the crisis was not basically a crisis born of the wartime devastation. It was a crisis of capitalist over-production, from which only the Soviet Union and the newly formed socialist countries of eastern Europe could claim immunity.

In a Labour Party policy statement, issued in 1950 under the title *Let Us Win Through Together*, it was said: "The nation's greatest need is to export more, especially to North America, so that we can pay for enough food to eat, and enough war materials to keep our factories running." It was not only these things that had to be paid for, however. There were the wars in Korea and Malaya and the quarter of a million troops then deployed throughout the world. And why did we have to "export more especially to North America?" We could have achieved better results by exporting our manufactured goods to the socialist countries in exchange for food and raw materials that they would have been only too glad to have allowed us to import.

We were told to produce more, consume less and export more. We did just that. Between 1945 and 1950, the volume of production was increased by 50 per cent. During this period, the consumption of almost all foods except potatoes fell below pre-war levels. At the same time, the volume of exports increased by 75 per cent. In spite of this, earnings in relation to prices, that is to say in real terms, moved steadily downwards. And with this downward trend came cuts in social services.

The real reasons for Britain's crisis were to be found in the decline of the British Empire and the ascendency of American capitalism. The crisis was aggravated by the reactionary imperialist policy of Ernest Bevin. In vain did the Communist Party warn the Labour movementy that "unless it compels the government to change completely its foreign policy, which is simply a continuation of the imperialist line of the Tory party and of the reactionary monopoly capitalists, there can be no fundamental social progress in Britain."

In 1948, lend-lease was replaced by Marshall aid. It was thanks to this, explained the Labour leaders, that we did not have a million and a half unemployed in this country. It was a frightening figure in those days. There were, of course, strings attached to Marshall aid. Trade restrictions were imposed on Britain, and an American economic administrator opened his offices in London in order to supervise these restrictions. On the 10th February, 1949, he reported to the American Senate Foreign Relations Committee that in Britain "the housing programme has been quite seriously cut back; so has the health programme and so has the programme for education." The nation pulled in its belt and worked harder. In the next two years, production increased by 17 per cent; profits and interest rose by 24 per cent; and real wages went down by 3 per cent.

THE SOCIAL WAGE

Along with the wage-freeze and cuts in social services at home, there was an intensive drive to step up colonial exploitation as a means of aiding British recovery. This was imperialism at its worst. In the period from 1947 to the end of the Labour government in October, 1851, £996 million of British capital was exported to the so-called sterling area. In his *Crisis of Britain and the British Empire,* Palme Dutt wrote:

> It was primarily on this basis of ruthlessly intensified colonial exploitation that the deficit of £545 million on the balance of payments in 1947 was converted into a surplus of £6 million in 1949. The Korean War, rearmament and United States stockpiling shot up the price of colonial raw materials to dizzy heights in 1950, and thereby made it possible for Britain's surplus on the balance of payments to rise to £258 million in that year. This was actaully acclaimed by the Labour government's propagandists as a triumph of socialist recovery.... This triumph was short-lived.... The interruption of United States stockpiling led to a decline in the price of colonial raw materials and under-mined the basis of the exceptionally inflated colonial profits during 1950 and 1951. The Labour government, faced with rising discontent at home, abandoned the field and called the General Election of 1951, to hand over to the Tories to carry forward even more ruthlessly the same basic policy.

A major factor of the crisis that capitalism now found itself in, though not the root cause, was the upturn in military expenditure since the end of the Second World War. This was the one crucial fact that was never mentioned by any official economist. As Palme Dutt wrote: "It remained the grand guilty secret of the dying imperialist order." Fortunately we are wiser today. The growth and development of the peace movement in Britain, with all its faults, has at least produced a new breed of activists who insist on knowing these things and disseminating the facts. By 1952, increased armaments and the drive to war was already costing the British people £1,634 million. It was the heaviest arms burden in the world in proportion to its population: 10 per cent more than the USA and 67 per cent more than the Soviet Union. How did this affect the so-called "welfare state" we were hearing so much about in those days. In a broadcast on the 6th March, 1952, President Truman said approvingly: Take the British. They are down to 16 cents worth of meat a week. That makes a mighty small package when the butcher wraps it up. They would have more if it were not for the defence effort."

So much for the myth of the "social revolution" brought about by the Labour government of 1945-51. According to the December, 1950 issue of the *Banker,* two-thirds of all industrial shares were then held by 42,000 people, each with an income of more than £20,000 a year. So much for the loudly-proclaimed "redistribution of the national income."

The myth of the "welfare state" was exploded by an official report of the Marshall Plan Administration published in the *Economist* at the beginning of 1950. This showed that the then current "social services income" per working-class family, taking into account social insurance, national assistance, family allowances, housing subsidies, food subsidies, education and health, amounted to an average of 57 shillings a week, while the then current taxation per working-class family amounted to an average of 67.8 shillings a week. Thus the whole of the "social service income" was paid for by the workers, who also had to contribute a further 10.8 shillings a week towards relieving the tax burden on the capitalists.

The educational reforms planned at the end of the war had been cut to meet the rearmament programme. The National Health Service had been crippled by the refusal to build the health centres that were at one time described as the key to the service. No new hospitals had been built, although by 1951 there were more than half a million people waiting for hospital beds. The housing situation had become desperate. In the House of Lords on the 21st June, 1950, the Archbishop of York said: "I doubt whether there has been any time in the last hundred years when overcrowding has been so grave and the slums have been so disastrous." Commented Palme Dutt: "Bombing planes and battleships before homes. Tanks before schools. Atom bombs in preference to hospitals. Such has been the price of the imperialist war policy.

After the defeat of the fourth Labour government in 1951, the Tories were given another three terms of office under three different Prime Ministers - Churchill, Eden and Macmillan. Then, in 1964, after thirteen years of Tory rule, the Labour Party was given a fifth chance, under the leadership of Harold Wilson. True, his government had an overall majority of only four seats, but he was optimistic and promised a Britain that would be made great again through the predominance of science, technology and welfare. But it all ended up with a prices and incomes policy that did nothing to keep prices down, nor for that matter "incomes" - with the exception of wages. It brought an immediate increase in unemployment, and, after sixteen months, devaluation of the pound.

Nevertheless, in 1966, Labour was voted in again; this time with an overall majority of 98. But by 1968, Britain was again in crisis. The answer to this was threefold: devaluation, wage restraint and cuts in social services. Twenty-two Labour MPs refused to vote for the cuts and were suspended from the Parliamentary Labour Party for a month. Prescription charges, the abolition of which had been paraded as one of the great achievements of the third Labour government, were introduced for all but the young, the sick and the old. The raising of the school-leaving age was postponed; house-building was slowed down; and charges were made for school milk and school meals. Unemployment began to grow.

At an anti-Common Market meeting in Blackpool on the 29th September, 1968, Emanuel Shinwell said: "In 1966 we were returned to Parliament with a majority of 90. There had never been a better chance of developing socialism. The government threw away its chances of building socialism in Britain by its obsession with getting into the Common Market. It sealed its fate with the publication of a White Paper entitled *In Place of Strife* - yet another attempt to keep wages down - opposed in Parliament by left-wing MPs but supported by the Tories, who further proclaimed publicly that they would carry it further through the future Tory government that they hoped to establish after the anticipated defeat of the Labour government because of its anti-union legislation.

On the 18th June, 1970, the electorate duly obliged by returning a Conservative government with an overall majority of 30 seats. Edward Heath became the new Prime Minister. In due time the Heath government also foundered on the rock of wage restraint, brought down largely by the victorious strike of the miners in 1972 and Heath's inability to face them again in 1974 with his overall majority in Parliament reduced to 17 seats. But it was no great victory for Labour, which emerged from the general election of February, 1974, as the largest single party but in an overall minority of 33 seats. The new Labour government lasted until the following October, when it was re-elected with an overall majority of three.

The minority Labour government had assumed office at the beginning of a new crisis in capitalism. By May, 1975, unemployment in Britain had risen to more than a million, with millions more on short-time working. The universal panacea for such a crisis has always been for the government of the day, irrespective of its political hue, to cut public spending, limit wage increases and reduce production. Such a policy naturally leads to further erosion of the welfare services. In the five years from 1969 to 1974, 32,000 hospital beds were taken out of service and 121 hospitals were closed. In his April, 1974, budget, Denis Healey, the Labour Chancellor, reduced the allocation to the health service by £134 million, while Dr. David Owen, the Under-Secretary of State for Health, made it clear that there would be substantial cuts in hospital-building programmes. There were also cuts in the maternity services and increases in dental and opthalmic charges. In his April, 1974, budget, Denis Healey warned that the population must accept cuts in its living standards or face further unemployment and further cuts in public spending. In July, 1975, the Labour government published a White Paper in which it talked of introducing "cash limits" on local authority spending. Those authorities exceeding their limits would receive no government help and would have to make unplanned cuts in other sectors to

THE WELFARE STATE

make up the deficits.

The cuts announced in November, 1975, were implemented in February, 1976, by which time unemployment had risen to 1.6 million with estimates of over 2 million by the winter of 1977. But there was worse to come. On the 3rd May, 1979, the Thatcher government came into power. It was now no longer a question of fighting against the erosion of the welfare services. It was a question of fighting for their very existence. The whole system of public assistance in education, health, housing and social security was to be dismantled piece by piece. A new word had come into our vocabularies, a word that struck fear into the hearts of all who were dependent upon one or another of the services that had been described euphemistically in the past as the "welfare state." That word was "privatisation."

The Conservative Party had always stood for "the encouragement of personal responsibility" through an extensive system of charges backed by private health insurance. They have encouraged the growth of private health schemes, private hospitals and other private services. Now it is planned to give government grants to people wishing to send their children to private schools, to step up the sale of council houses, and to encourage people to take out their own insurances against unemployment, sickness and old age. Transport, be it by land, sea or air, is to be privatised. Telecommunications and shipbuilding are to be privatised. Everything that it is possible to privatise will be privatised if the Thatcher government has its way. In the process of implementing this policy, unemployment has risen to three million officially but nearer to four million in reality. Is this, the "welfare state?" There are some who still think so, even among our own class. The promotion of home ownership and the payment of large sums of redundancy money has lulled some of our better paid brothers into a false sense of security. Among those workers who can still afford cars, television sets, washing machines and even home computers and videos, there are those who have been anaesthetised by the media and believe they are actually receiving the full fruits of their labour. They cannot see that despite these cushions, they are still being robbed of their surplus value. The rude awakening will come when the redundancy pay has been spent, or lost in some uneconomic business enterprise; when the consumer credits have been exhausted and when all their proud possessions have been repossessed.

The heavy burden of the armaments programme is an ongoing problem. It looms larger now than ever before. It is forecast that in 1984 we shall have to find more than 16 billion pounds to meet its insatiable appetite. This will mean more cuts in our welfare services. The armaments programme is the biggest single unproductive drain on our resources. Is it the same all over the world? What is the situation in the socialist countries in this respect? Let us turn to the text of a speech made by Konstantin Chernenko, General Secretary of the

THE SOCIAL WAGE

Communist Party of the Soviet Union and now President of that country. Speaking to the voters of the Kuibyshev constituency in Moscow, he said, on the 2nd March, 1984:

> In the last five years complications in international affairs have forced us to divert sizable resources to meet needs related to strengthening our country's security. But even in these circumstances we have never even contemplated any cutting back of social programmes.

This speech was made during the recent elections. Here in Britain we know so little about the Soviet Union that most of our compatriots are not even aware that there have been elections this year in which considerably more than 90 per cent of the adult population took an active part. We know that there is soon to be an election in the USA for a new President, but not that there has been an election in the Soviet Union for a Supreme Soviet. This is not accidental. In those capitalist countries where its leaders are pledged to a policy of military domination, even at the expense of their own peoples, it would not advance their cause to allow the truth to be revealed to their own masses regarding the activities of the peace-loving socialist states.

Since the end of the Second World War, and indeed since long before that, there have been, from time to time, massive movements in Britain for better social conditions and higher wages. Sometimes the workers have made advances, but these advances have usually been lost in the counter-offensives of the employing classes that have followed them. For instance, the miners made big advances in their wages and conditions in 1972 and 1974. But where are those advances now? They have all been eroded. Similarly, the Beveridge plan, when it was first introduced, brought great advantages to those who most needed help. But those advantages have now all gone the way of the miners' wages. Is there any point then, in giving our lives to the struggle for better wages and conditions if we are to lose out again as soon as the heat of the struggle passes? Karl Marx had something to say on this subject in an article of his in the New York *Daily Tribune* on the 14th July, 1853, which read, in part, as follows:

> The alternative rise and fall of wages, and the continual conflicts between masters and men arising therefrom are, in the present organisation of industry, the indispensable means of holding up the spirit of the labouring classes, of combining them into one great association against the encroachments of the ruling class, and of preventing them from becoming apathetic, thoughtless, more or less well-fed instruments of production. In a state of society founded upon the antagonism of classes, if we want to prevent slavery in fact as well as in name, we must accept [class] war. In order

rightly to appreciate the value of strikes and combinations we must not allow ourselves to be blinded by the apparent insignificance of their economical result, but hold in view above all things, their moral and political consequences. Without the great alternative phases of dullness, prosperity, over-excitement, crisis and distress, which modern history traverses in periodically recurring cycles, with the up and down of wages resulting from them, as with the constant warfare between masters and men closely corresponding with those variations in wages and profits, the working classes of Great Britain and all Europe would be a heartbroken, weak-minded, a worn-out unresisting mass, whose self-emancipation would prove as impossible as that of the slaves of ancient Greece and Rome.[2]

Eighteen years later, on the 23rd November, 1871, Karl Marx wrote, in a letter to Bolte:

Where the working class is not yet far enough advanced in its organisations to undertake a decisive campaign against the collective power, that is the political power, of the ruling classes, it must at any rate be trained for this by continual agitation against the policy of the ruling classes and adopting an attitude hostile to it. Otherwise it will remain a plaything in their hands.[3]

When you hear such passages as those quoted above, it is hard to realise that there are people in our movement today who would have us believe that Marxism is an outdated concept, that the great works of Karl Marx have no relevance in modern society. Would that Tommy Jackson were alive today to apply his scathing wit to the outpourings of these false prophets who seem to have dedicated their lives to the denigration of the works of Marx and Engels, the founders of scientific socialism.

Social welfare under capitalism, i.e., unemployment and sickness benefits, retirement and old-age pensions, rent and rate rebates, education, subsidised transport etc. etc. is all part of the social wage. It is just as much a part of the subsistance that the average worker lives on as the money wage. That being so, the same properties must apply. And our attitude towards the struggle to increase the social wage must be the same as our attitude towards the struggle to increase the money wage. In the struggle to increase either the money wage or the social wage, the working class learns how to organise in trade unions and political parties and, hopefully, how to organise itself for the final seizure of state power.

---

[2] *Collected Works,* Marx and Engels, Vol. 12, page 169.
[3] *Selected Works,* Marx and Engels, Vol. 2, Pages 423-424.

THE SOCIAL WAGE

In times of capitalist affluence, the better-organised workers will be able to win improved social conditions and higher wages, but in times of capitalist crisis, they will lose some of the advances they made in better times. The social wage will therefore fluctuate, as the money wage will, from one period to the next. The real gains of the struggles of the workers to rise above their subsistence levels are not the increased wages in themselves, but the lessons that are learned about the power of working-class unity and organisation, and the ultimate lesson that permanent gains can only be made by changing the system of society. To reap the full fruits of their labours, the workers must take control of state power and use it to build socialism. Only then will they be able to enjoy a continuously rising standard of living through higher money and social wages. There can be no such thing as a welfare state under capitalism. The welfare state is, in fact, the socialist state.

In the days of Marx, there was no socialist state that he could point to as a living example of the system of society that he knew would replace the capitalist state. But he knew it would come. We, on the other hand, are privileged to be living in the era of transition from capitalism to socialism. I said at the beginning of this lecture that I would return to the subject of the true welfare state later. If you want to know what a welfare state is, look to the Soviet Union. There they have been building a welfare state for the past 67 years, for the past 54 of which they have not known unemployment. The last Labour Exchange in the Soviet Union closed its doors for ever in 1930. Just consider, no one in that country under the age of 67 has ever known unemployment. Under Article 40 of the Constitution of the USSR, citizens have, and I quote: "the right to work (that is guaranteed employment and pay in accordance with the quantity and quality of their work, and not below the state-established minimum), including the right to choose their trade or profession, type of job and work in accordance with their inclinations, abilities, training and education, with due account of the needs of society. This right is ensured by the socialist economic system, steady growth of the productive forces, free vocational and professional training, improvement of skills, training in new trades or professions, and development of the system of vocational guidance and job placement."

This is the key to all the welfare services that are enjoyed by citizens of the Soviet Union, and have been so enjoyed in ever-increasing measure since 1930. Remember my quotation from William Gallacher, which I introduced at the beginning of this lecture: "The right to exploit the people for profit cannot be tolerated if there is to be social security." Exploitation for profit leads to unemployment; and Gallacher forecast that the so-called "welfare state" of William Beveridge would collapse when unemployment assumed mass proportions. Is this not what is happening today in Britain? But exploitation for profit was abolished for all time in the socialist sixth of the world with the advent of

THE WELFARE STATE

the Great October Revolution of 1917. With the subsequent abolition of unemployment, it became possible to lay the foundations of a true welfare state.

Now Soviet citizens also have the right to rest and leisure, under Article 41 of the Soviet Constitution; the right to health protection (Article 42); the right to maintenance in old age, in sickness, and in the event of complete or partial disability (Article 43); the right to housing (Article 44); the right to education (Article 46). Of course, they also have responsibilities: to work conscientiously in their chosen, socially useful occupations, and strictly to observe labour discipline (Article 60); to preserve and protect socialist property ... to combat misappropriation of state and socially- owned property (Article 61); to safeguard the interests of the Soviet state (Article 62); to respect the national dignity of other citizens (Article 64); and (under Article 69) to promote friendship and co-operation with the peoples of other lands and to maintain and strengthen world peace.

There are other rights enjoyed by Soviet citizens that have not yet been incorporated in the Soviet Consitution but are enjoyed nevertheless. They are the right to cheap transport, subsidised food and subsidised holidays. Eventually, when production reaches the required level, and when socialist man has thrown off the last vestiges of his capitalist past, all these things will be free. Lenin defined socialism as a system of society wherein each gave according to his ability and received according to his work. Communism he defined as a system of society wherein each would give according to his ability and receive according to his needs. This already applies to the very young, the sick and the old. Given the required level of production and the nurturing of the social consciences of Soviet citizens along socialist lines, it will eventually apply to everyone. And that will be as near to the perfect welfare state as we can hope to reach. When will that be? Probably a little longer than I think; but a great deal sooner than some others in my audience might imagine.

What then is the task before us? We must fight every inch of the way for better wages and conditions, and for better welfare services. We must fight to protect our hospitals and schools and old people's homes and other social institutions. But in so doing, we must never forget that we can only make permanent gains if we also fight to change the system of society so that we can begin to build socialism in Britain. For there will be no true welfare state in this country until we end the system of exploitation for profit that leads only to overproduction, unemployment and war. To the fulfilment of these noble aims, Tommy Jackson devoted his whole life, his abundant skills and his unquenchable spirit. Let us go forth and do likewise.

Note: The above lecture was delivered on the 23rd May, 1984, before counter-revolutionary elements within the Soviet Union had come out openly

THE SOCIAL WAGE

in favour of a return to a capitalist market economy. How it was possible even to think of this within a society already enjoying the basic needs of life, while large sections of the working class in the capitalist countries went short and millions in the third world starved, will be discussed in the second part of this book.

MATERIAL AND MORAL INCENTIVES

Their Role in the Construction of a SOCIALIST SOCIETY

SO FAR THERE HAS BEEN very little critical examination of the politico-economic history of the Soviet Union with a view to establishing the root causes of the deterioration of its socialist system into a capitalist market economy. A start has been made, however, with the publication of two books, both written around the end of the 1980s and now available in Britain. They are *Perestroika: A Marxist Critique* by Sam Marcy, and *Che Guevara: Economics and Politics in the Transition to Socialism* by Carlos Tablada. Both deserve to be read and studied by a much wider public than is the case at present.

It is my endeavour, in this section of my book, to relate the ideas expounded by Marcy and Tablada to the role of the social wage as the main moral incentive for change in the transition from socialism to communism.

It should be stated at the outset, in case there should be any doubt about it, that both the authors of these books take as their guide the classic works of Marx and Engels, from which they continually quote. In the very first chapter of his book, *Economics and Politics in the Transition to Socialism* Carlos Tablada notes that according to the writings of Ernesto Che Guevara on the period of transition to socialism and communism, there are two elements that are "indissoluably linked" in the theoretical works of Marx and Engels. They are the *economic* relations within the production process and the *social* relations established both inside and outside the production process.

Tablada also notes that these two elements, which were separated by bourgeois theoreticians and by the social democrats of the Second International, were reunited by Lenin in the course of building the first proletarian state power - though separated again today by some contemporary theoreticians. Commenting on this. he says:

> The divorce of these two elements since the time of the Second International has produced the most colossal distortion that the theory of Marx and Engels has ever been subjected to. It constitutes a return to pre-Marxist philosophical positions. This regression drives a wedge between revolutionary theory and practice - neither of which, without the other, can retain its revolutionary power and potential.

THE SOCIAL WAGE

Tablada shows how Che Guevara defended this, and other important principles of Marxist-Leninist economic theory relevant to the period of transition to communism, in the light of "new factors arising from the socio-economic and political system in which he lived;" and that therein lay his originality. He believed that although *material incentives* would be necessary for some time, *moral incentives* should be the fundamental lever for building socialism in human society.

Che Guevara constantly stressed the importance of correlating the transformation of the social relations of production with the transformation of the political and social consciousness of the working people carrying out this revolutionary process. "To build communism," he wrote in *Socialism and Man in Cuba*, published in 1965, "it is necessary, simultaneously with the new material foundations, to build the new man." Social attitudes towards work and incentives had to be changed. Participation in Sunday voluntary work mobilisations on needed social projects, for instance, was a good example of the type of selfless contribution that lies at the base of conscious progress towards communism.

In a speech given in October, 1987, Fidel Castro pointed out that after the departure of Che Guevara from Cuba in 1965, no serious attempt was made to put his ideas into practice and the accumulating errors confronting Cuban Communists had to be corrected later. These errors began to be apparent during the 1970s. Had they not been corrected they could have become irreversible.

A tendency to want money to regulate everything began to take hold. "We began paying very high wages and salaries that had no relation to what was being produced," said Castro in an interview with a reporter from the French Communist newapaper *L'Humanité*, in May, 1987. "Awards, bonuses, and overtime payments multiplied.... We were beginning to fall into a trend that would undermine the revolutionary spirit, the consciousness of our workers."

Castro also cited a number of mechanisms borrowed from capitalism that had been gaining increased acceptance in Cuba: distribution of food and other necessities through the market with prices determined by supply and demand; evaluation of economic performances of state enterprises by their *profitability* rather than by their production of socially necessary goods; increasing reliance on bonuses and individual material incentives while expenditures on the *social wage* (housing, health, education, day care) stagnated, thus widening social inequalities.

It is relevant to point out that a similar situation had arisen in Czechoslovakia in the early 1960s, when, after a period of rapid advancement, its economic development had begun to slow down. Looking back on this period in his introduction to the *Czechoslovak Statistical Abstract for 1971*, Dr. Jan Vecer wrote:

MATERIAL AND MORAL INCENTIVES

Some of the Czechoslovak revisionists-economists began to see the reasons for the slow-down to lie in the way in which the national economy was being managed. They started to press for a gradual decentralisation of management, and under-estimated planning. In principle this was nothing less than an imitation of the state existing in the capitalist countries. Some authors even started to consider the creation of a reserve army of unemployed and an arrangement under which enterprise risk would have a direct effect on the working people in the individual plants. They tried to solve the temporary economic difficulties, at the cost of the working people, mainly by raising the cost of living. They also created the impression that Czechoslovak economic difficulties could not be solved without a foreign loan, which should be granted to Czechoslovakia by some West-European country. Other economists stressed the favourable impact of inflation on economic growth, and attempted to introduce an inflationary policy into practice. The independence of the enterprises, the weakening of the planned management of the national economy, free prices and slow inflation became the main postulates of economic policy in 1968-69.

These economic policies, however, only succeeded in aggravating the difficulties. Inflation led to price increases and to demands from the workers for higher wages. These were granted and the costs recovered by further price increases. These, in turn, led to more increases in wage rates, which began to rise more quickly than productivity. And this led to a shopping psychosis with everyone trying to spend their money before it became devalued. In this situation a market economy began to emerge.

It has to be said that the process of correcting these errors was more painful in Czechoslakia than it was in Cuba, where they had not been allowed to take such a hold. But in both cases moral incentives had begun to give way to material incentives and the social wage sacrificed in order to raise the money wage.

An even more serious situation had developed in Hungary some years earlier where, in spite of a rise of 50 per cent in the national income between 1949 and 1953, real wages had actually fallen by 16 per cent, mainly as a result of attacks on the social wage. This had led to open counter-revolution in 1956 with grave consequences for the world communist movement. The full story, which has many resemblances to the recent situation in the Soviet Union has been told elsewhere.[4]

---

[4] See *Hungary 1919 and 1956: The Anatomy of Counter-Revolution* by Ernie Trory; still available from Crabtree Press Limited, 4 Portland Avenue, Hove, East Sussex BN3 5NP. Price: £1.80 including postage.

THE SOCIAL WAGE

In an interview with Jean Daniel of the Paris *L'Express*, given in Algiers and published on the 25th July, 1953, Che Guevara said:

> A socialist economy without communist moral values does not interest me.... One of the fundamental aims of Marxism is to eliminate material interest, the factor of individual self-interest and profit, from man's psychological motives. Marx was concerned both with economic facts and with their reflection in the mind, which he called "a fact of consciousness." If communism neglects facts of consciousness, it can still serve as a method of distribution but it will no longer express revolutionary moral values.

Marxists in capitalist countries readily accept that the *objective conditions* for revolutionary change, i.e., unemployment, homelessness, poverty and so on, do not automatically lead to the transfer of power from the ruling capitalist class to the working class. They agree that the *subjective conditions* have to be there as well: that there has to be a conscious desire on the part of the workers, led by a vanguard party in which they put their trust, before the old system can be replaced. Marxists must now learn to accept that in the transition from socialism to communism, the objective conditions for realising this aim, i.e., full employment, good housing conditions, plentiful supplies of food and adequate productive wealth in all departments, even masses of consumer goods, will not automatically lead to communism. Here again, the *subjective conditions* have to exist as well. There has to be a conscious desire for transition to the higher stage of society on the part of the workers, led by a vanguard party in which they put their trust and with which they are prepared to work selflessly for its realisation. Only then will it be possible to expect everyone to give according to his or her ability without specific individual rewards and to receive according to his or her needs. It is the duty of the vanguard party to inspire and foster this selfless desire so that the transition from socialism to communism can be achieved.

Of course, in the early stages of socialism, material incentives will be necessary. Marxists recognise this when they work for a system ensuring that all workers receive the full fruits of their labour; that in exchange for work according to their ability they receive payment in accordance with the quantity and quality of their work. But during this stage, one might say especially during this stage, the vanguard party must make it a priority to educate its followers in the need to promote the moral and social values that alone will ensure the transition from socialism to communism.

The sacrifices made by the Soviet peoples between the wars, in order to convert their country from a backward peasant economy into an industrial giant, and the sacrifices made by them in their struggle to drive out the invaders during the war, presuppose a high standard of social consciousness. The same can be said of the socialist countries that emerged as a result of their liberation from the nazi occupiers. But somewhere along the line, they lost their revolutionary consciousness; and without it all hope of transition to a higher form of society vanished.

In the event, the vanguard parties failed to arouse in the workers the revolutionary zeal that was essential to their further progress. They found it difficult to achieve, perhaps did not even realise that it was necessary, and so failed to cut the umbilical cord that bound them to capitalist ideology.

Cuba, in the early years of its revolution, was no exception to this general rule; but thanks to the theories developed by Che Guevara and taken up by Fidel Castro, it corrected its mistakes and now shows no sign of following the road recently trod by the Soviet Union and the other ertswhile socialist countries. Unfortunately, lying only 70 miles from the USA, and no longer protected by the Soviet Union, Cuba is vulnerable to attack from its powerful neighbour. It could fall to armed intervention from the USA if the international working-class movement fails to come to its aid. But unless it again changes direction it will not fall to the lure of consumerism.

There has been much talk in recent months of the validity of the law of value. Che Guevara rejected this and other capitalist categories, including the market and even money, as the guiding principle in the period of transition to communism. He spoke of the need for economic policies that tended towards the gradual withering away of these levers of direct self interest. He believed that the law of value, as Marx defined it, was a phenomenon of capitalist society, and that it could not be applied in the period of transition to communism. Or, as Tablada puts it:

> Even in the period when commodity production still exists as a sector of production, the *law of value* no longer governs completely. Measures taken by a socialist state, such as the lowering of rents through subsidised housing, the provision of medical care and social assistance, either free of charge or at prices below those set by the market, the control of prices in order to combat counter-revolutionary speculation, to achieve control over foreign currency and to eliminate unemployment make it impossible for the *law of value* to operate. It ceases to be a regulatory mechanism with the character of a law. Prices are no longer set by market fluctuations. In this stage distribution is established, not on the basis of value, but in accordance with the political programme.

Of course, no society can consume more than it produces or imports. That is self-evident. But, to use Tablada's exact words: "socialism can permit itself the luxury - impossible for capitalist society - of setting prices above or below the value of a particular item."

In a capitalist society, the value produced by the workers for which they are not paid, Marx called "surplus value." This is expropriated by the capitalists and used partly to improve their own standards of living, partly to replace the capital (constant and variable) that has been used in its production, and partly to expand and develop the means of exploiting a larger number of workers. In a socialist society, this value, which I prefer to call "extra value" since it is not expropriated, is returned to the workers throughout the country in full in the form of improved social services, free education and health care, and subsidised housing, food and transport.

This is what we call the "social wage" as distinct from the "money wage." When the people realise that the social wage is more important than the money wage, they will have raised their conscious desire for the transition to communism to a level that will make it possible. The social wage benefits everybody. The money wage benefits only the recipient and his or her family. To work for others as for oneself and to be motivated by a desire to see a general improvement in the quality of life from one end of the country to the other, and indeed throughout the world, is absolutely essential before mankind can move on from socialism to communism. Let each give according to his or her ability. Under socialism the reward will be found partly in the money wage, reflecting the value of the work performed in the process. Under communism the reward will be found only in the social wage, reflecting the needs of everyone. But the desire to progress to this higher stage has to be there before it can be achieved. And if such a society does not progress, is not orientated towards this higher goal, it will at first stagnate and then deteriorate.

This is the lesson that the peoples of the erstwhile socialist countries failed to learn. Their concentration on the money wage, in the later stages of their existence, led to a selfish desire for more and more consumer goods *at any price*. They took for granted the rewards they had achieved in the past and consolidated in the high standard of their social wage. They saw only the apparent profusion of luxury consumer goods enjoyed by those living in the West and imagined that to be the lot of everyone under capitalism. They did not realise, or they did not care, that the capitalists, the better-off professional classes and the top grade workers in the West, only enjoyed their relatively high standards of living at the expense of the poorer-paid workers and the unemployed in the metropolitan countries, and of the starving millions in their colonial dependencies that had been exploited and robbed of their mineral wealth for hundreds of years and were now having to grow cash crops for export instead of food for their populations in order to meet the demands for interest on development loans they would never be able to repay.

The agents of the imperialist powers played a not inconsiderable part in encouraging this situation. But if the vanguard parties in the erstwhile socialist countries, including the Soviet Union, had understood their true roles they could have won their people to a realisation of the actual state of affairs in the capitalist countries and in the third world and taught them to appreciate the value of their own considerable social achievements. In so doing they could have pointed the way forward to the higher stage that we call communism.

Instead, in order to satisfy the demands of their peoples for the consumer goods that were available in the capitalist countries for the minority who were able to pay for them, the socialist countries allowed themselves to be drawn into a mad scramble for "hard currency." This opened the way for "concessions" to transnational companies that were able to move in and exploit the local workers.

Despite the fact that there was little or no unemployment in the socialist countries, the capitalist companies that took advantage of the concessions granted to them had no difficulty in obtaining employees. Because of their high social wage, the money wage of the local workers was low. The capitalist companies simply offered them more money. This was, of course, less than the capitalist companies would have had to pay in their own countries. And since the socialist workers employed by the capitalist companies were no longer contributing "extra value" to the common pool, though still enjoying the benefits of their social wage, the workers in the socialist enterprises were, in fact, subsidising the money wage of those employed by the capitalist companies.

In the West, the social wage, which was continually under attack, was quite small and dwindling. It was devalued in respect of the National Health Service for instance, by raising prescription charges, instituting charges for dental treatment and for eye tests and driving people in need of urgent hospital treatment to resort to private practices. It was further devalued by privatising road transport and forcing up fares, and by privatising gas, water, electricity and telephones.

In the socialist countries, all such services were provided either free of charge or at heavily subsidised prices. There a family of workers would pay no more than five per cent of their earnings in rent, whereas a family of workers in the West would have to pay up to 30 per cent of their combined incomes in rent or sometimes even more in mortgage repayments. In the USSR food prices, because of subsidies, had remained static for 20 years or more, whereas in the West, food had to be paid for at continually rising market prices. In Moscow, a worker could travel from one side of the city to the other for five kopecks, about five-pence in English money. How far could a worker in London travel for that amount?

THE SOCIAL WAGE

Subsidies are part of the social wage, whether in a capitalist or in a socialist country. The social wage reflects the security afforded to the worker. It is not a coincidence that in the socialist countries, where the social wage was high, there was full employment, whereas in the capitalist West, where the social wage is small, there is the constant threat of unemployment. Child-care, free education and the right to old-age pensions are all part of the social wage. There was a marked contrast between their relative values in the socialist countries as compared with the capitalist countries. The social wage was always higher and the money wage always lower in the socialist countries than in the capitalist countries.

The plain fact is that if, in the socialist countries, the social wage had continued to cover more and more human requirements, the money wage would have had less and less significance and would finally have disappeared. In the capitalist countries it is the social wage that is being eroded. This is now also the case in the erstwhile socialist countries that have recently embraced the capitalist ethic. It is true that the money wage in these countries is increasing; but unfortunately for their citizens, the money wage is not increasing at the same rate as the social wage is decreasing.

When Gorbachev first became General Secretary of the CPSU he allowed it to be believed that he was only interested in extending democracy, reducing bureaucracy and drawing more and more people into the government of the country in order to strengthen socialism. In a speech given in Moscow on the 7th November, 1987, on the occasion of the 70th anniversary of the Great October Socialist Revolution, he said: "We see again and again that the socialist option of the October Revolution has been correct.... The year 1917 showed that the choice between socialism and capitalism is the main social alternative of our epoch, that in the 20th century there can be no progress without advance to socialism, a higher form of social organisation."

He praised the wisdom of Lenin in launching his New Economic Policy; and few were then able to see that he was, in fact, about to advocate a return to those days of retreat, which Lenin emphasised were only of a temporary nature. Yet the clues were there. "These days we turn ever more often to the last works of Lenin," said Gorbachev ambiguously, "to Lenin's New Economic Policy, and strive to extract from it all the valuable elements that we require today."

Yet he could still say: "The period after Lenin, that is the '20s and '30s, occupied a special place in the history of the Soviet State. Radical social changes were carried out over 15 years. An incredible amount was squeezed into that period - both from the point of view of searching for optimum variants of socialist construction, and from the point of view of what was really achieved in building the foundations of the new society."

In recalling the struggle of the party against the "leftist, pseudo-revolutionary rhetoric" of Trotsky, and noting that he was "acting in common with the new opposition headed by Grigori Zinoviev and Lev Kamenev, Gorbachev asserted that "the party's leading nucleus, headed by Joseph Stalin, had safeguarded Leninism in an ideological struggle." Of the great events of the '30s, later the subject of much bitter recrimination in the former Soviet Union, Gorbachev said:

> Looking at history with a sober eye, considering the aggregate of internal and international realities, one cannot help asking whether a course other than that suggested by the party could have been taken in those conditions. If we wish to be faithful to history and the truth of life, there can be only one answer: no other course could be taken.

In explaining the basic principles of *perestroika*, Gorbachev described its purpose as "the full theoretical and practical re-establishment of Lenin's conception of socialism, in which indisputable priority belongs to the working man with his ideals and interests, to humanitarian values in the economy, in social and political relations, and in culture." Most members of the various communist parties throughout the world accepted Gorbachev at face value. It was left to Margaret Thatcher, the most reactionary Tory prime minister that Britain had seen for a long time, to recognise that Gorbachev was "a man she could do business with."

But even as long ago as 1987, in the speech already quoted, he spoke with two voices. On the one hand he declared: "The world communist movement grows and develops upon the soil of each of the countries concerned, but there is something that the image of a communist has in common, no matter what his nationality is, no matter what country he works in." But a few paragraphs later he was saying: "The time of the Communist International, the information bureau, even the time of binding international conferences is over." Further on still he was declaring: "Comrades, the emergence of the world socialist system is the most important landmark in world history since the October Revolution." But this was conveniently forgotten when he toured the socialist countries urging them to adopt *perestroika* and move with the Soviet Union towards a market economy.

He concluded his address on the 70th anniversary of the October Revolution with the words: "In October 1917 we parted with the old world, rejecting it once and for all. We are moving towards a new world, the world of communism. We shall never turn off that road." But less than four years later, on the 17th April, 1991, in a speech to businessmen in Japan, he emphasised the need for the Soviet Union to "switch to market relations in order to be able to co-operate with other countries." Now the accent was all on "material incentives." Moral incentives no longer mattered. The social wage was unimportant. What mattered was personal income, i.e., the money wage. "We are creating favourable conditions for entrepreneurship," he said, "moving away from monopoly production and rigid economic state administration in order to replace centralised distribution with free wholesale and retail trade." Later in his speech, Gorbachev announced with pride:

> I want you to know that about 50 per cent of consumer goods and up to 40 per cent of capital goods are now priced on market principles in my country. A short while ago, things were very different, with nearly everything regulated by the central authorities. Thus, in a matter of a year of two, we have made a great leap forward.... Recently, the federal legislature passed a law on entrepreneurship in the USSR. This law allows the existence of state-run, collective, leased and private enterprises, joint stock companies and co-operatives. Privatisation and transferring state-run enterprises on to a joint-stock basis is also being planned.

On the subject of a farming-reform programme, he had this to say: "Moves are under way to ensure that, together with collective farms that will work on new market-based principles, private farming develops in accordance with general market laws. We have had extensive discussions, which are still in progress, on the future of collective farms: the question is whether or not they should all be disbanded and replaced with private farms." Regarding concessions to foreign companies, Gorbachev assured his listeners: "The relevant presidential decree sets out important provisions on this score and allows businesses owned entirely by foreigners to be set up in the Soviet Union."

One might ask: When did the USSR give up its conscious struggle for the transition from socialism to communism? Gorbachev told the world when it did NOT, when he informed his Japanese colleagues:

> In the Second World War, we did not just lose 27 million human lives. The entire European part of our country was devastated and the health of the nation was severely undermined. Despite predictions that we would not get back on our feet again even after a hundred years, we did; and not only did we stand up again, but we also managed to accomplish monumental tasks of scientific and technical progress. This attests to the high potential of our society and of the nations that make up our land.

The achievements of the Soviet peoples, both during the Second World War and in the period of reconstruction that followed, bear testimony to the spirit of selflessness that was a feature of those difficult days. The remarkable feats of first winning the war and then rebuilding their country could not have been performed if the "What's in it for me?" attitude that later pervaded the atmosphere in the USSR had existed in those trying times. The people then were ready and willing to make sacrifices in pursuit of a common cause.

That being so, it is illogical to pretend that Stalin, who was still leading the USSR until his death in 1953, was responsible for all the ills that now beset the relics of that once proud country. Stalin made many mistakes in a very difficult period but he could not have been responsible for the destabilisation of the socialist system, for that was not accomplished until long after his death.

In a speech to the Japanese Parliament, also delivered on the 17th April, 1991, Gorbachev tried to explain his "new thinking." In doing so, he referred to "the collapse of the Berlin Wall," which, he said, borrowing an expression first used by Dr. Goebbels, "put an end to the *iron curtain* in Europe." He went on to speak of "a readiness to take into account new realities, and of reliance on everything that is viable and leads to more stable and mutually advantageous relations." These vague criterea "of the new relations, which are now taking shape among countries also in the eastern part of Europe," he was convinced, were factors "acting in the interests of the world community as a whole."

Of the Gulf war, he said: "It is deplorable that force had to be used. But the aggressor left no other choice for the United Nations." He pointed out that "the Gulf crisis affected the vital interests of many states, including the Soviet Union and Japan." But he failed to mention the more obvious interests of the United States. Many regard the failure of his representatives in the United Nations to use their veto to prevent the outbreak of war as the ultimate betrayal of the trust of working people all over the world. And that in a futile search for accomodation with US imperialism.

Returning to the subject of *perestroika* towards the end of his speech, Gorbachev asked what had been achieved in the six years that had passed since it was first introduced. "We have set about changing relations of ownership and have begun to make the transition to a mixed market economy," he said. "We shall promote enterprise in every way, support initiative in business." And finally: "The world has been built in such a way that rich and poor people are bound to exist in it for a long time yet." This was a statement worthy of becoming his epitaph.

Just as it was expected that in the transition from socialism to communism man would also change himself, so in the regression from socialism to capitalism it is equally expected that man will again change himself - this time from a social being motivated by high moral and social incentives, to a self-seeking individual, motivated only by the "powerful material incentives" upon which Gorbachev was relying for the success of his *perestroika*.

Happily, there are other socialist countries still in existence in other parts of the world that have not yet succumbed to the "new thinking;" and even if they are defeated there will be others that will arise from the ashes of the "new world order" to challenge this so-called "new thinking," which, as Graucho Marx might have said, "is old thinking already."

George Blake, imprisoned in Wormwood Scrubs in 1961 for passing information to the Soviet Union, but escaping in 1965 and living in Moscow in 1990, where he saw the Soviet system collapsing around him, attributed its failure, in his autobiography, *No Other Choice,* to the fact that "neither in this country, nor anywhere else, have people at the end of the twentieth century grown to the moral stature required to build a communist society;" nevertheless adding confidently, "but of one thing I am certain: mankind will return to this experiment, it will try again. Now here, then there, it will make new attempts to build communism, for deep inside us - all of us - there is an instinctive yearning for it."

APPENDIX I

Speech Made to the Sixth National Congress of the New Communist Party of Britain on the 12th December 1987

IN HIS SPEECH on the occasion of the 70th anniversary of the October Revolution, Gorbachev devoted only a few minutes of his very long speech (a column and a half of the 48 columns of the complete text published by *Soviet Weekly* on the 7th November) to the subject of the world communist movement, and none of it addressed to the very real problem of how to combat the dead hand of Eurocommunism that is holding back the advance of socialism in a number of countries throughout the world.

On page xv of the text published by *Soviet Weekly*, Gorbachev speaks of "loyalty to the idea of a communist society, loyalty to the working people - above all the working class," but he makes no mention, in that section, of loyalty to the principles of Marxism-Leninism, although on page iv, in his historical introduction, he mentions that after the death of Lenin "the party's leading nucleus, headed by Joseph Stalin, had safeguarded Leninism in a ideological struggle," and that "the victory of the socialist revolution would have been impossible without a party equipped with the Marxist-Leninist theory." Yet he failed, in his speech, to give recognition to those new Marxist-Leninist parties that have been founded in various parts of the world for the precise purpose of safeguarding Leninism and of organising working people in parties equipped with the Marxist-Leninist theory that they require to become vanguard parties of the working class.

In the issue of *Soviet Weekly* published on the 14th November, it is reported that "180 parties and movements from countries throughout the world, who had come to Moscow to attend the 70th anniversary celebrations" were present at a meeting of "world progressives" in the Kremlin. At that meeting, Gus Hall, general secretary of the Communist Party of the USA, a man whom we all respect, said that he wanted to remind comrades from countries where there is more than one communist party, "that division within their ranks weakened the struggle against imperialism." But he offered no solution to the problem. Or, if he did, it was not reported. Surely the solution lies in understanding the reason why new Marxist-Leninist parties had to be formed in those countries where the old communist parties had taken up a reformist stance. The New Communist Party of Britain, alas, was not represented among the "world progressives" who met in the Kremlin. In a report in *Soviet Weekly* of the activities of foreign guests

THE SOCIAL WAGE

in the Soviet Union during the 70th anniversary celebrations, top billing was given to an address by Gordon McLennan to workers at the Stankoagregat.

At the 40th Congress of the Communist Party of Great Britain, Viktor Zorkaltsev, the fraternal delegate from the CPSU, called upon the British Communists to solve their current difficulties "using scientific Marxism-Leninism as a guide." His call fell on stoney ground. Zorkaltsev, according to *7 Days,* won applause "when he described *perestroika* as the struggle against everything old and obsolete." Obviously many of the delegates regarded this as recognition of their own revisionist policies, and of the belief of the leadership of their party that Marxism-Leninism was foremost among those things "old and obsolete" that had to be discarded. Many of the members of the CPGB believe that the CPSU is being restructured along Eurocommunist lines. This is probably what they were applauding. In vain did Zorkaltsev conclude: "Let the decisions of your congress further the interests of the working class." Most of the true Marxist-Leninists and nearly all its leading working-class members have now been expelled from the CPGB. There was a list of the latest batch on page 5 of the *Morning Star* on the 17th November. As Peter Geddes wrote in the *New Worker* on the 20th November, in the last paragraph of his report: "Caught as it is between political and financial bankruptcy, the Communist Party of Great Britain confirmed at its 40th Congress that it is now of almost total irrelevance to the problems confronting the working class."

By continuing to give recognition to a party pursuing disruptive policies in the peace movement, and anti-Soviet and anti-working-class policies in all its activities, the CPSU runs the risk of bringing discredit upon itself.

Meanwhile, the *Morning Star* remains a paper without a party, aspiring only to become the paper of the broad left, a useful role as far as it goes and one that we can support, but no substitute for a Marxist-Leninist party with its own newspaper. The responsibility for uniting the Marxist-Leninist elements of the communist movement in Britain falls upon the shoulders of the New Communist Party. The result of the 40th Congress of the CPGB justifies, if justification were still needed, the action taken by the founders of the NCP 10 years ago. I am proud to have been a foundation member of the New Communist Party. It is time that the Communist Party of the Soviet Union and Marxist-Leninist parties everywhere gave us the recognition we have earned.

Let the CPSU answer our call and take the lead in promoting a World Conference of Communist and Workers' Parties, and let the newly-formed Marxist-Leninist parties in those countries where the old communist parties are no longer pursuing Marxist-Leninist policies, be among the first to be invited.

APPENDIX II

Speech made to the Seventh National Congress
of the New Communist Party of Britain
on the 9th December, 1989.

I WANT TO SAY A FEW WORDS about the leading role of the party, not only as part of the process of analysing what is happening in Europe, but also because there are vital lessons here for us in Britain.

As you know, the question of the leading role of the party has become a very serious issue in communist and workers' parties all over the world. Let me say at once that I believe most steadfastly in this as an incontrovertible Marxist-Leninist principle. I believe, however, that it is a position that has to be won. Moreover, it is not a position that can be won once and for all time, but one that has to be won over and over again, every day and every minute of every hour of every day.

That being so, I do not believe that a Marxist-Leninist party, after becoming the ruling party in any country, can perpetuate its leading role by inserting a clause to that effect in its country's constitution. It is not as simple as that. It has to maintain its leading role by its honest and wise counselling, by the example of its leading members and by its day to day contact with the people. Its leading role cannot be maintained by legislation. The events now taking place in Europe are proof of this. Such a role can only be maintained by the assent of the masses it purports to lead.

Recently, Karel Urbanek, general secretary of the Communist Party of Czechoslovakia, said: "Today, the party wants to set out on a new course. This will be very difficult because we can only work if we have the confidence of the people. Right now, we don't have that confidence and authority."

It is not enough, and it never will be enough, for a Marxist-Leninist party, having successfully led the working people of a given country to a position of power, to assume that it has the right to that leading role for all time without proving itself in every complex situation that arises thereafter. To attempt to consolidate that role by including it in the constitution is, in my opinion, an act of bureaucracy institutionalising complacency: a recipe for stagnation and, at worst, corruption.

Such I believe to have been one of the causes of the present situation in a number of those socialist countries in Europe where communist and workers' parties are now being asked to give up their leading roles. Comrades, they gave up their leading roles when they started taking them for granted. Now, they have to try to win them back before their countries are plunged into counter-revolution. And when they do, they must never again lose faith in the masses.

In the *History of the Communist Party of the Soviet Union (Bolsheviks) - Short Course*, published in 1939, it is stated on the authority of Lenin: "All revolutionary parties that have hitherto perished, did so because they grew conceited, failed to see where their strength lay. . . ." but a party is invincible if it is able "to link itself with, and to a certain extent if you like, to merge with the broadest masses of the toilers."

In an article on *Defects in Party Work* also quoted in the *Short History*, Stalin tells the story of Antæus, a hero of Greek mythology, who was invincible all the time he maintained contact with his mother earth, which gave him strength. He was undefeated in battle until he met Heracles who lifted him from the ground and throttled him. "I think," wrote Stalin, "that the Bolsheviks remind us of . . . Antæus. They are strong because they maintain connection with their mother, the masses, who gave birth to them, who suckled them and reared them. And as long as they maintain their connection with their mother, with the people, they have every chance of remaining invincible.

That is the main lesson we must learn from the mistakes that have been made in the past, during the period that Gorbachev has described as the period of stagnation, a period during which some of the leaders of the communist and workers' parties in the Soviet Union and in the socialist countries relied on their "legal right" to the leading role of their parties and lost contact with the masses.

I am confident that the Communist Party of the Soviet Union will retain its leading role; and that soon there will be a turn in the fortunes of the country it still leads. Then the revisionist ideas that have permeated large sections of the communist movement in so many of the socialist countries will be recognised as irrelevances and unceremoniously discarded.

Comrades, we may be a long way away from realising a leading role for our party in this country. But that is our aim and it may come sooner than we think. These days can be as years in the essence of their concentration. But, whether sooner or later, it is not too early for us to learn that once won our leading role will have to be maintained, not by an Act of Parliament but by our words and deeds.

This, of course, is true of leadership in general. It applies to the leading role of the working class, to the role of our party in the vanguard of the working class, and to the leading role of our Central Committee and its officers within our party.

And may I take this opportunity of congratulating our Central Committee on the statement it recently produced on international issues and published in the 17th November issue of the *New Worker*. Such a statement could not have been produced by a body that had lost contact with the masses.

If we draw our strength from the working people around us; if we listen to them and win their confidence and trust; if our party becomes their party, we will march together to the conquest of power. And having done so, providing we do not allow ourselves to be separated from them, we shall have no need to legislate for the perpetuation of our leading role.

We hear much today about "new thinking" and "old thinking." Comrades, it is not a question of "new thinking" versus "old thinking;" it is a question of "right thinking" versus "wrong thinking."

The resolution of our Central Committee, already referred to, recognises that there are, in the socialist countries, forces that want change in order to weaken socialism as well as those who want change in order to strengthen it, and that these forces are in contention. Overshadowing this struggle are the charges of corruption now being levelled against some of the old leaders. If these charges are proved, the culprits deserve the severest of punishments.

Here in Britain, we are used to hearing about corruption. It is an integral part of capitalism, particularly in its present critical stage. But we are not used to hearing about corruption in the socialist countries. Such corruption is a thousand times worse since it is not an integral part of socialism. It damages, not only the country in which it occurs but the whole of the world communist movement. Charges have been levelled and will be pursued but we should not assume in advance that these charges are already proven.

Nor should we, or the workers living in the socialist countries, believe that the West is interested in solving the problems of socialism. The hand of the CIA and the influence of the British Tory government are clearly discernible in Poland and Hungary, where it is widely believed that capitalism has something to offer them. But the problems of socialism can no more be solved by a reversion to capitalism than can the problems of capitalism be solved by a reversion to feudalism.

Most disconcerting of all is the retreat from history. The recent declaration of the Warsaw Pact countries that it was wrong to come to the aid of Czechoslovakia when she was threatened by counter-revolution in 1968 may be "new thinking" but it is not "right thinking." Have they forgotten the plans for a counter-revolution organised by the American CIA, under the code name of "Prague Spring," involving the infiltration of Czechoslovakia by trained commandos disguised as tourists while the West German regular army carried out its "Black Lion" manoeuvres on the West German border with Czechoslovakia.

Two years have elapsed since our last National Congress, when I criticised the Communist Party of the Soviet Union for failing to respond to the call for a World Conference of Communist and Workers' Parties. I make that plea again today. The upheavals in Europe are the concern of communists worldwide; they should be called together to discuss the present situation. And we should be there

THE SOCIAL WAGE

to put our point of view. Failing that, we ourselves should take the initiative and call a world conference of those Marxist-Leninist parties that are not afraid to stand up and be counted in these difficult times.

APPENDIX III

Article published in *DISCUSSION*
on the 28th February, 1991, under the title
CONSUMERISM AND ANARCHY

WRITING IN the *Guardian* on the 9th February, Walter Schwarz, its religious affairs correspondent, condemned the dependence of individual societies on ever-higher levels of comfort, personal mobility and consumption: levels that can be achieved only by the privileged in our societies, and be maintained only by the domination and exploitation of the Third World.

He saw the need for cheap oil to fuel this consumerism as being a root cause of the conflict in the Gulf, and went on to say that we need to simplify our way of life, conserve energy and diversify its sources, divert employment from luxuries to community services, favour public over private transport ... and give priority to sharing and service over the endless growth of individual consumption.

Commenting on this in its editorial of the 11th February, the *Morning Star* correctly pointed out that this was a programme for radical social change and as such incompatible with capitalism. Despite the exploitation of the Third World, only a relatively small section of the working class in the West has been able to enjoy the benefits of consumerism, while at the other end of the scale, homelessness, unemployment, a low level of education and an inferior health service has become the order of the day.

There is a lesson here for socialist societies of the future. If successive post-war Soviet governments had appreciated this more fully, and acted upon it by explaining to its peoples what was happening in the West through its preoccupation with consumerism, they might not have been led into involving their country, and the other countries of the then-socialist world, in the mad scramble for hard currency that was to become a major factor in their destabilisation.

In the pre-war world, the economy of the Soviet Union forged ahead while capitalism slumped into a crisis from which it only recovered through the expansion of its war industry. In the Soviet Union, the workers gave freely of their time in subbotniks and valued their achievements in agriculture and industry. They believed that full employment, guaranteed homes (however basic), good education and a free health service for all were more important than holidays abroad and consumer luxuries for the few. Their social consciousness was their motivation.

The onset of consumerism in the socialist countries, after the end of the

THE SOCIAL WAGE

Second World War, led to the adoption of a capitalist morality and ultimately to the demand for a market economy that it was hoped would enable their populations to achieve the standards they believed existed for everyone in the West.

The recent collapse of the market economies in the erstwhile socialist countries, including the Soviet Union, can now only be seen as a part of the general break-up of capitalism into anarchy and war.

If we are ever to move forward to socialism in Britain, we must learn from the mistakes made by the post-war socialist governments of Europe and equip ourselves with a more fundamental understanding of Marxism-Leninism. When the workers come to power in Britain, as I believe they will, they must be sure of vanguard party that is able to resist the blandishments of consumerism until basic standards of living are secured all over the world.

APPENDIX IV

Article published in the *New Worker* on the 7th June, 1991, entitled *THE EIGHTEENTH BRUMAIRE OF MIKHAIL GORBACHEV*

ON THE 9TH NOVEMBER 1799 (the 18th Brumaire in the French revolutionary calendar), the republican government was overthrown by a coup d'état and Napoleon Bonaparte placed at the head of affairs as First Consul and virtual dictator of France.

When Louis Bonaparte, a nephew of Napoleon Bonaparte, overthrew the constitution on the 1st December, 1851, as a preliminary to having himself crowned Emperor Napoleon III a year later, Karl Marx responded with a work entitled *The Eighteenth Brumaire of Louis Bonaparte*. In this work Marx drew an ironical comparison with the events leading to the crowning of Emperor Napoleon I.

The circumstances in which the Supreme Soviet of the USSR gave President Gorbachev the right to rule by decree on the 24th September, 1990, and later, on the 19th October, a mandate to substitute a "market economy" for centralised socialist planning, fully justify the title chosen for this article.

In *The Eighteenth Brumaire,* Marx draws the attention of his readers to Hegel's remark that "all facts and personages of great importance in world history occur twice" and goes on to add a remark of his own to the effect that they occur "the first time as tragedy, the second as farce."

There is no reason, however, to believe that such events "in world history" are limited to two appearances. After all, Oliver Cromwell had his "18th Brumaire" when he assumed the title of Lord Protector and now Mikhail Gorbachev has had his. But if Napoleon Bonaparte appeared on the scene as tragedy and Louis Bonaparte as farce, how is one to describe the appearance on the scene of Mikhail Gorbachev?

Like all of Marx's important works, *The Eighteenth Brumaire* deserves to be read again in the light of contemporary events in the Soviet Union and in the rest of the erstwhile socialist countries. "From 1848 to 1851," Marx tells us, "only the ghost of the old revolution walked about ... An entire people, which had imagined that by means of a revolution it had imparted to itself an accelerated power of motion, suddenly finds itself set back into a defunct epoch, and in order that no doubt as to the relapse may be possible, the old dates arise again, the old chronology, the old names, the old edicts, which had long become a subject of antiquarian erudition, and the old myrmidons of the law, who had seemed long

THE SOCIAL WAGE

decayed."

Certainly in the Soviet Union today there are ample signs of the return to a "defunct epoch" - the old flags, the old religious festivals, and the old place names.

Comparing the revolution of 1848 with the revolution of 1789, when each of the parties engaged relied successively on the next most progressive party for support and thus moved the revolution "along an ascending line," Marx wrote of the later revolution: "The proletarian party appears as an appendage of the petty-bourgeois-democratic party.... The democratic party, in its turn, leans on the shoulders of the bourgeois-republican party.... The bourgeois-republicans ... support themselves on the shoulders of the Party of Order. The Party of Order ... throws itself on the shoulders of armed force.... The revolution thus moves in a descending line."

The coup d'état of Louis Bonaparte was advertised well in advance of the event. As early as the 29th January, 1849, barely a month after his election as President of the Republic, Louis Bonaparte had made a proposal about it to General Changarnier.

During every parliamentary crisis, the Bonapartist journals had threatened it and during the months of September and October, 1851 rumours of a coup d'état had followed thick and fast.

On the other hand, the coup d'état of Mikhail Gorbachev had hardly been discussed at all before the 21st September, 1990 when, according to a report in the *Guardian* on the following day, President Gorbachev had threatened "to close down elected bodies and impose presidential rule if the situation in parts of the Soviet Union ran further out of control."

A few days later, on the 25th September, the *Guardian* was able to announce: "President Gorbachev won special powers from parliament yesterday to impose by decree whatever market reform he chooses." And on the 20th October, the *Morning Star* reported that on the previous day, the Soviet leader "gained the political mandate needed to begin on the hazardous path of restructuring the country's crisis-ridden economy by a crushing 356 votes to 12 against."

The passage from democratic government to rule by presidential decree may have been sudden but the signs had been there for a long time. The first to recognise the potential of the new general secretary of the Communist Party of the Soviet Union (CPSU) was Margaret Thatcher who, having met him soon after his election, declared at once: "He is a man I can do business with." To our shame, we laughed at the idea.

Our suspicions were aroused, however, when he resisted all requests to call a world conference of communist and workers' parties. In no time at all he had persuaded the CPSU to give up its vanguard role and to drop the idea of the dictatorship of the proletariat. He cancelled practically all aid to the Third World and encouraged the spread of bourgeois ideologies by allowing a variety of political parties to be set up, some of which had strong racial overtones.

But while turning his back on proletarian internationalism, he gave support to the aims and objects of bourgeois internationalism by opening his doors to capitalist investment, by accepting loans, by granting concessions and by generally paving the way for a full-blown market economy.

In explaining their failures, Marx says of the proletarian revolutions of the nineteenth century in his *The Eighteenth Brumaire* that they "criticise themselves constantly, interrupt themselves continually in their own course, come back to the apparently accomplished in order to begin it afresh, deride with unmerciful thoroughness the inadequacies, weaknesses and paltrinesses of their first attempts, seem to throw down their adversary only that he may draw new strength from the earth and rise again, more gigantic before them, and recoil again and again from the indefinite prodigiousness of their own aims, until a situation has been created which makes turning back impossible.... As ever, weakness had taken refuge in a belief in miracles, fancied the enemy overcome when it had only conjured him away in imagination, and lost all understanding of the present in a passive glorification of the future in store for it."

There is no need to add another word of explanation in order to apply this gem of Marxism to the present situation, though Marx would have wondered how it was that we had still not learned the lessons he taught 140 years ago.

By the same author:

BETWEEN THE WARS
IMPERIALIST WAR
WAR OF LIBERATION
SOCIALISM IN GERMANY
HUNGARY 1919 AND 1956
POLAND IN THE SECOND WORLD WAR

Serious students of the current political situation will find the information contained in the above books imperative to a thorough understanding of the collapse of socialism in the Soviet Union and in the eastern and central European countries where it had appeared to flourish. Those who are fortunate enough to have these books in their libraries should re-read them in conjuction with a study of this pamphlet. Those who do not already possess them should send at once for a price list while the books are still available. Write now to Crabtree Press Limited, 4 Portland Avenue, Hove, East Sussex BN3 5NP.

Notes

Notes